Ja
D

by Brian Platt

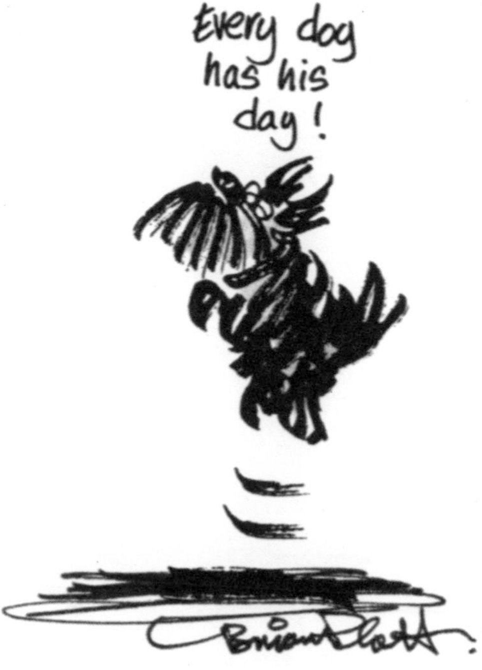
Every dog
has his
day!
Brian Platt

Published by Accent Press Ltd – 2005
www.accentpress.co.uk
ISBN 0954867327
Copyright © Brian Platt - 2005
The rights of Brian Platt have been asserted.

Printed and bound in China

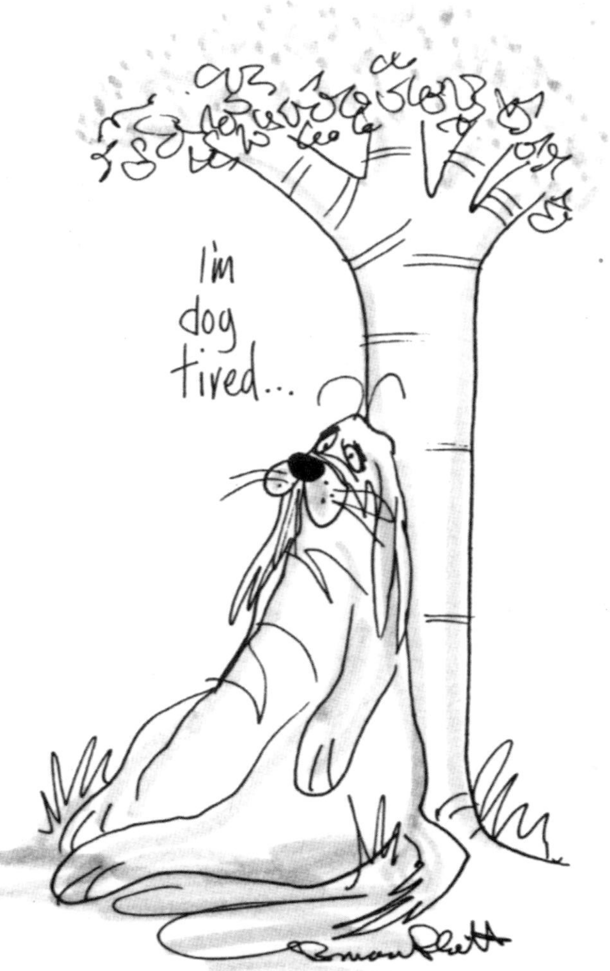
I'm dog tired...

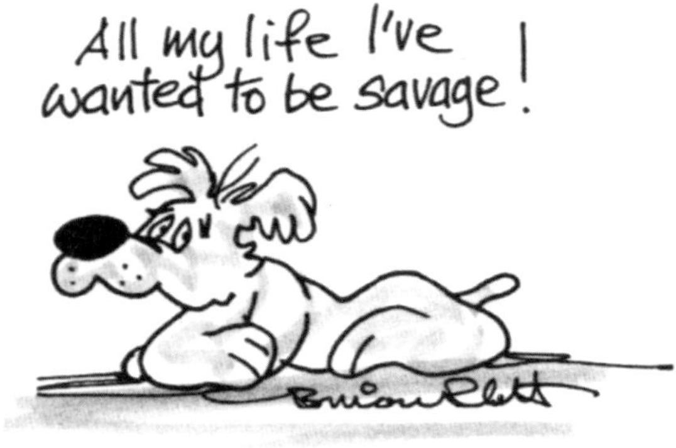
All my life I've wanted to be savage!

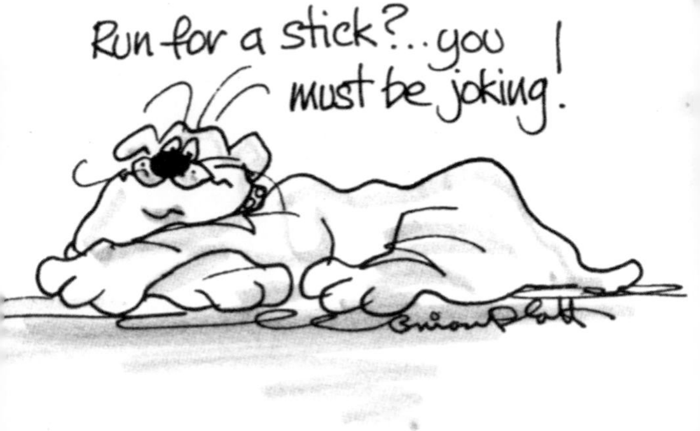
Run for a stick?...you must be joking!

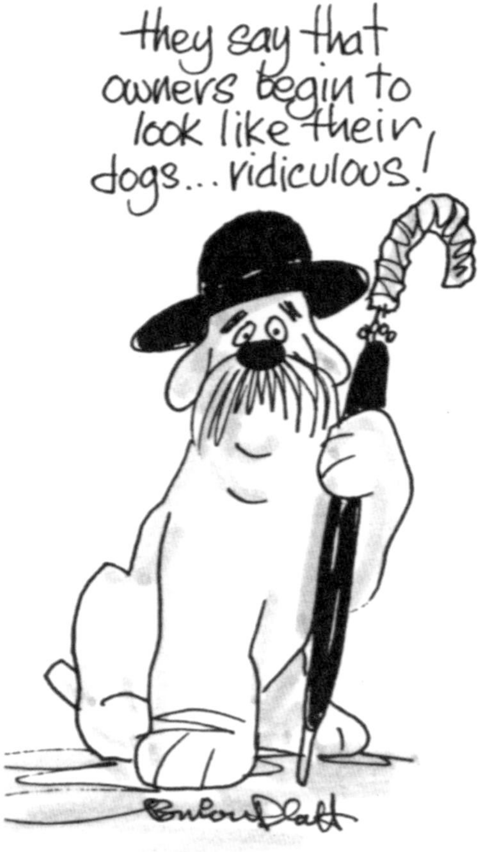
they say that owners begin to look like their dogs... ridiculous!

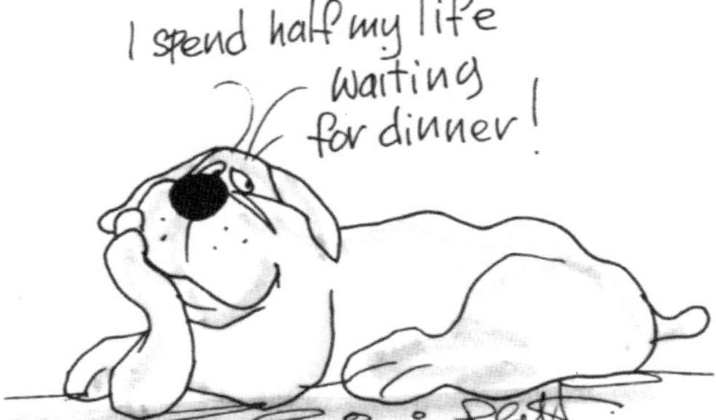
I spend half my life waiting for dinner!

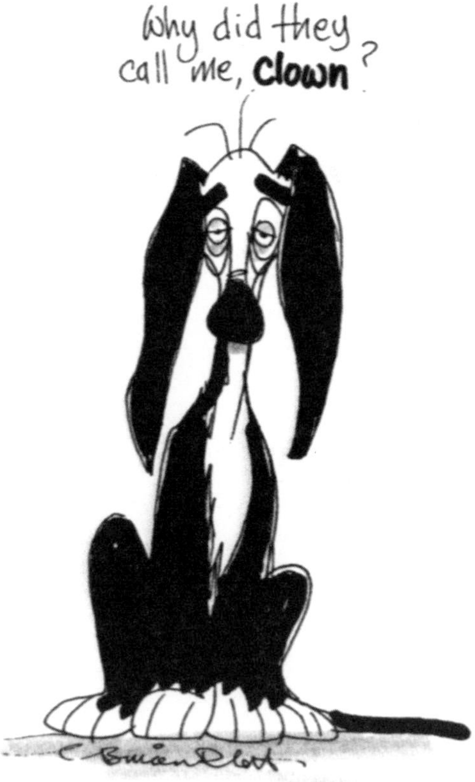
Why did they call me, Clown?

twirling
ears is
what I'll
do!

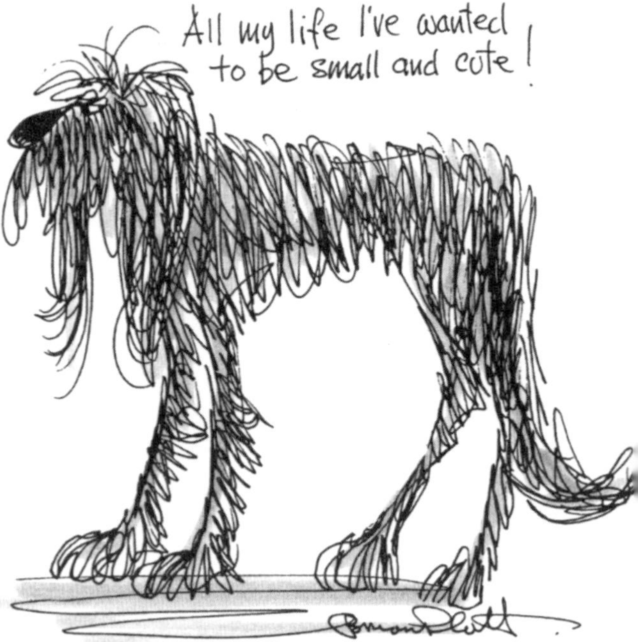
All my life I've wanted to be small and cute!

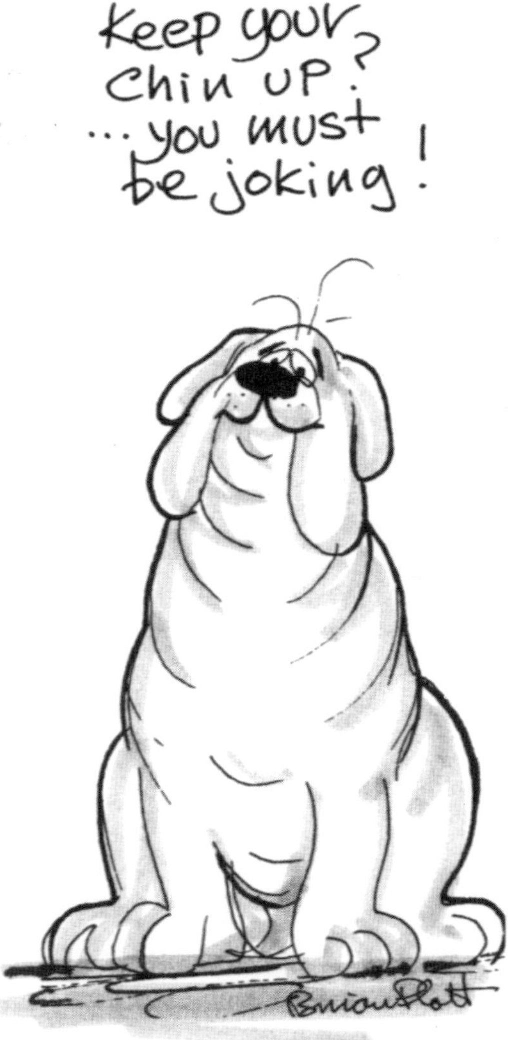
Keep your chin up?
...you must be joking!
Brian Platt

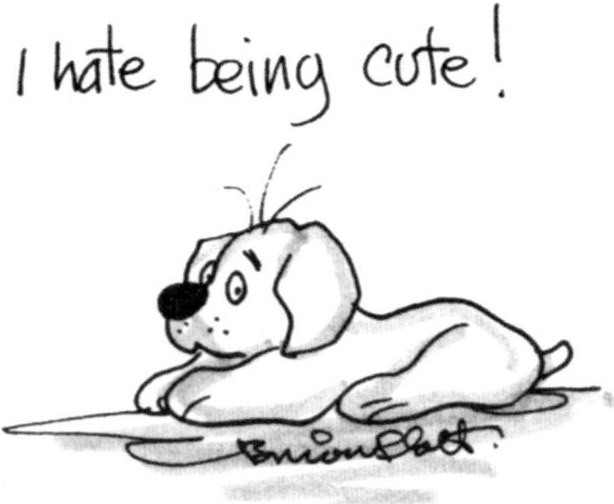
I hate being cute!

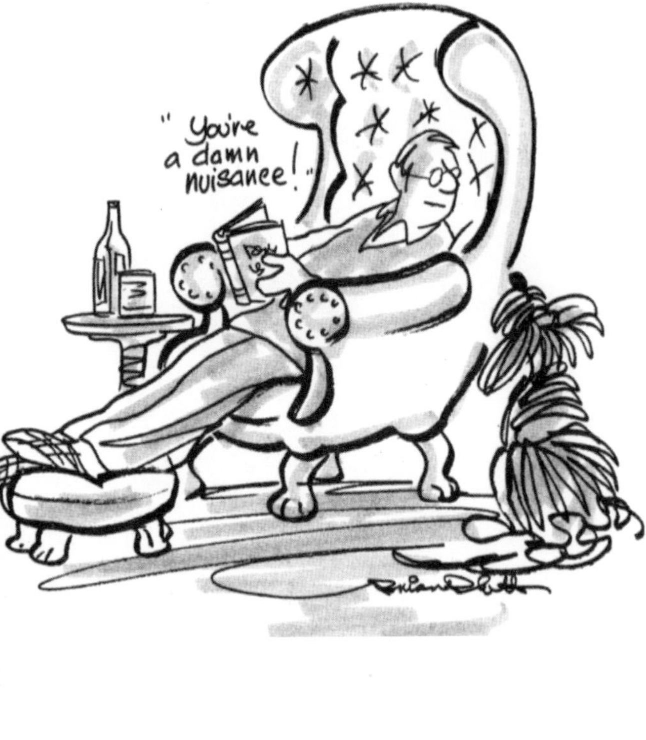
"You're a damn nuisance!"

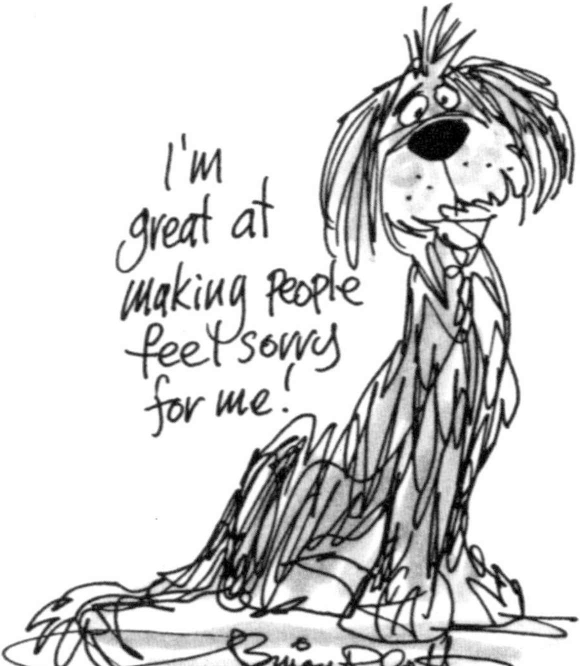
I'm great at making people feel sorry for me!
Brian Platt

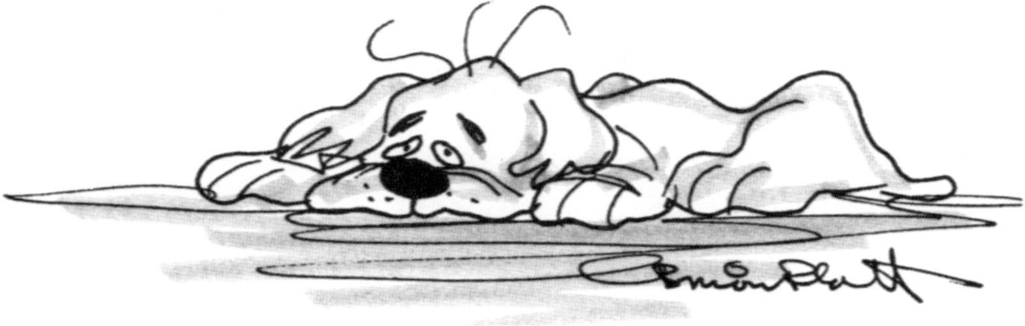

I'm not gonna' do a damn thing today!

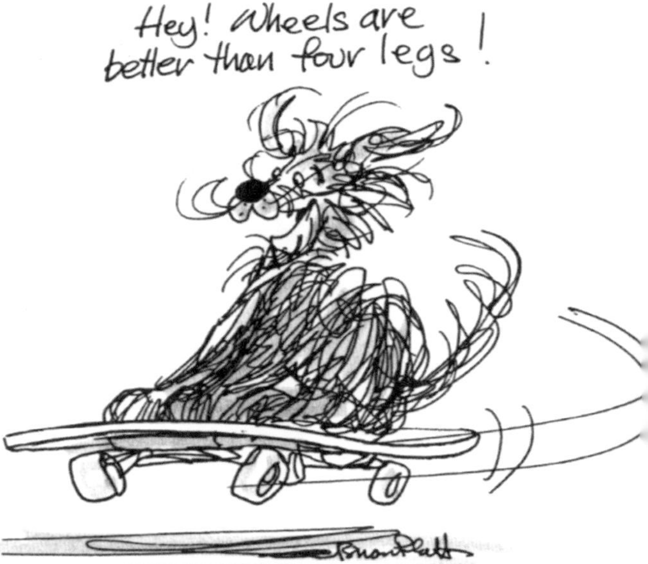
Hey! Wheels are better than four legs!

I'm about as low as I can get!

they've found it!

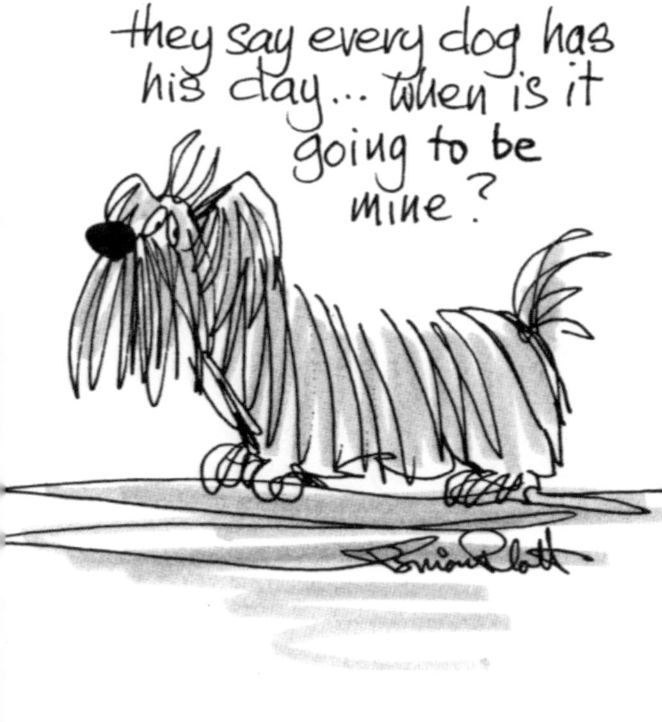
they say every dog has
his day... when is it
going to be
mine?

Did I hear the sound
of a tin-opener?

I hate cats...

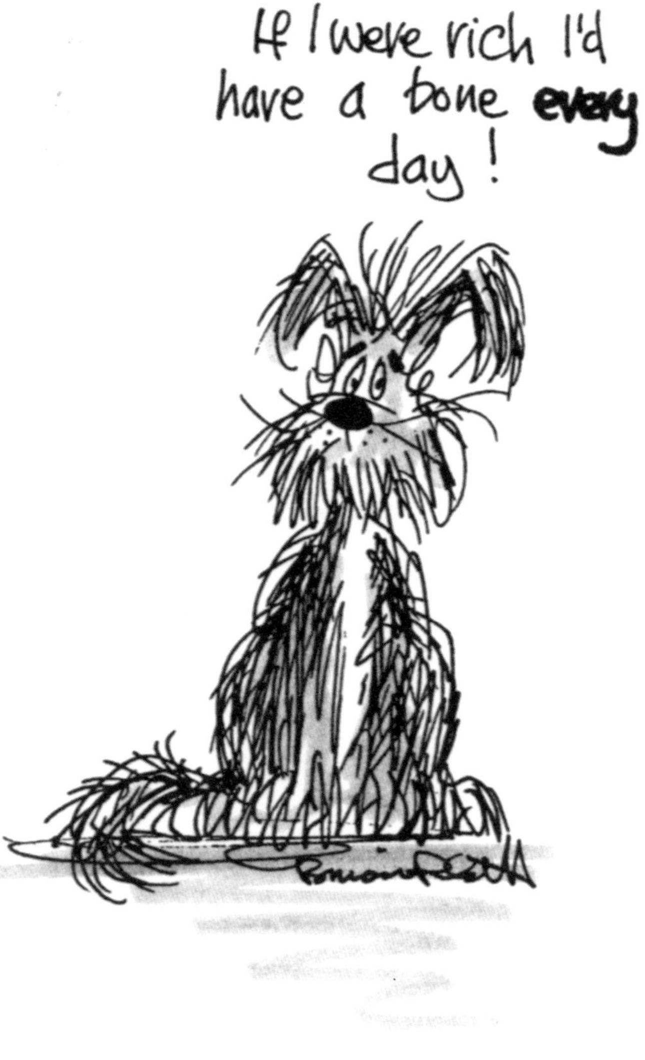
If I were rich I'd have a bone every day!

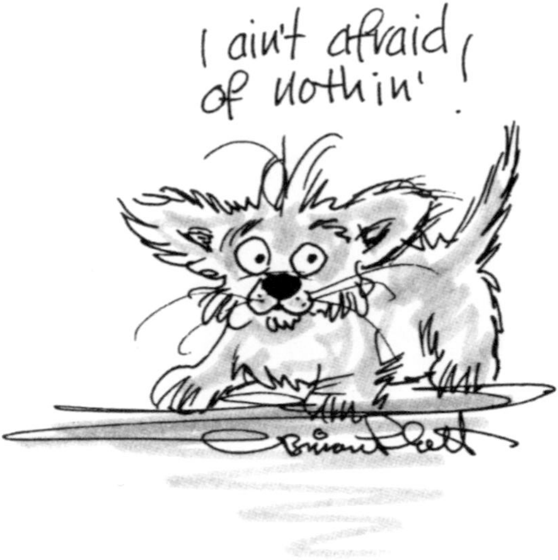
I ain't afraid of nothin'!

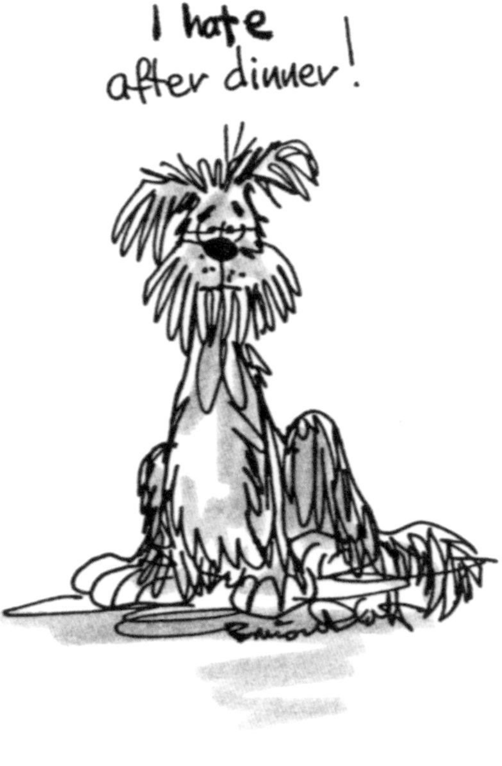
I hate
after dinner!

oh no... not another walk!

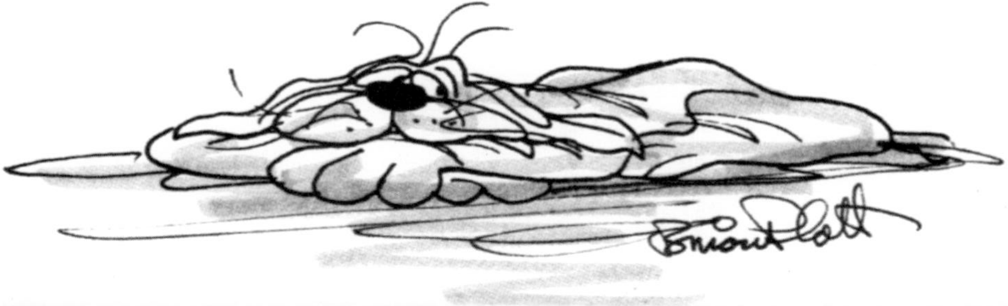

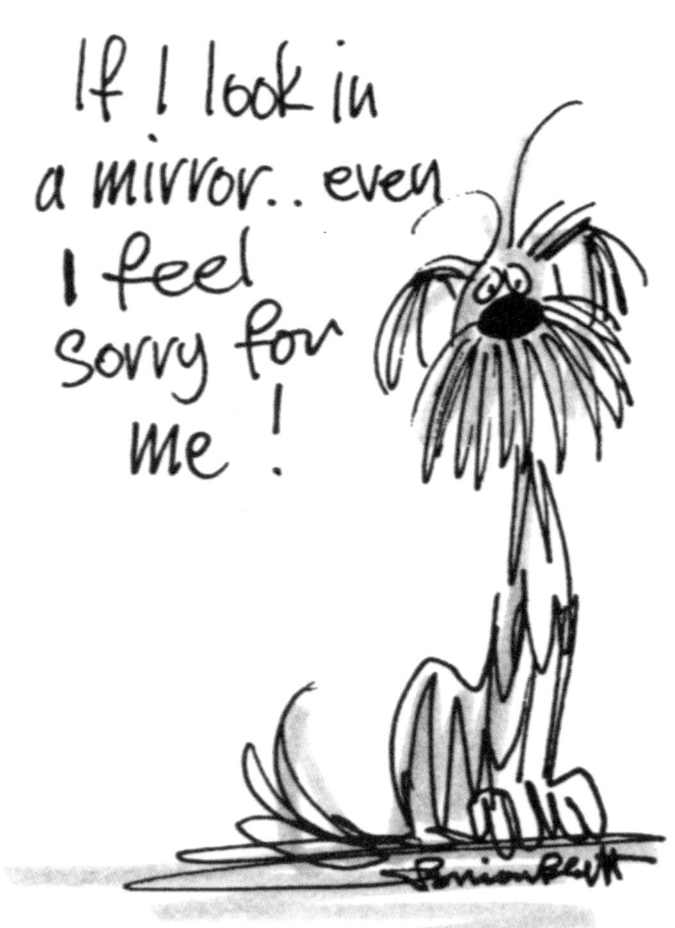
If I look in a mirror.. even I feel sorry for me!

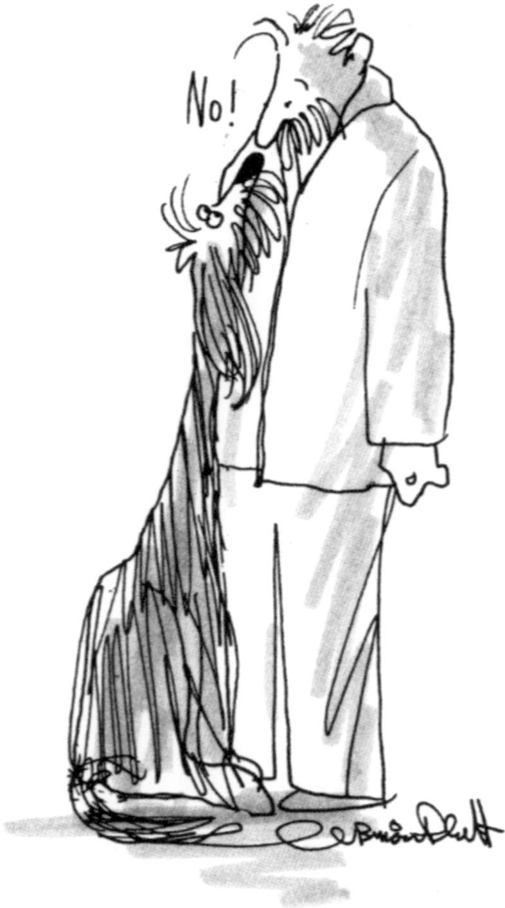
No!

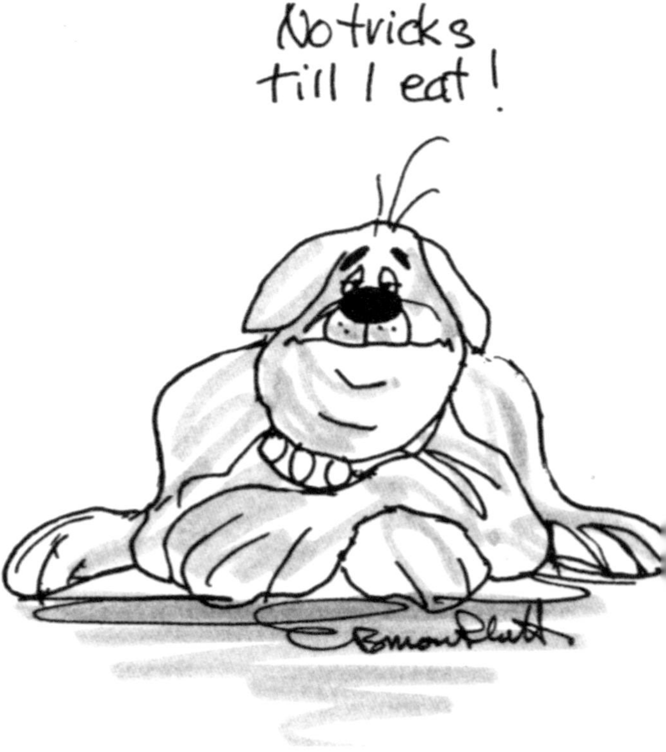
No tricks
till I eat!

only foor more hours till dinner!

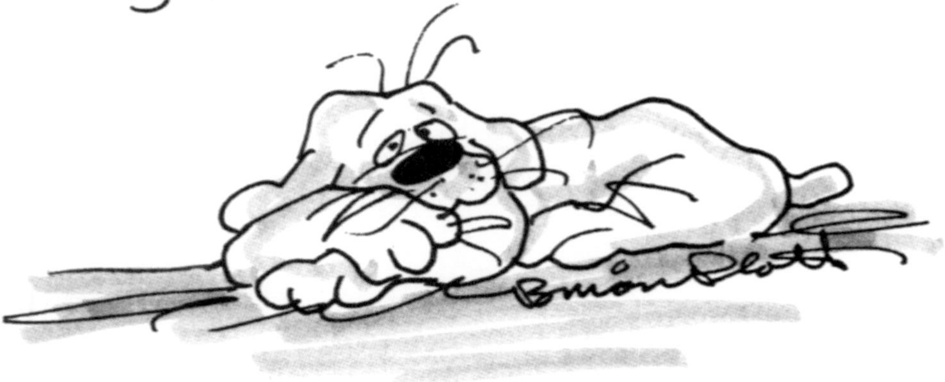

Begging is an art!

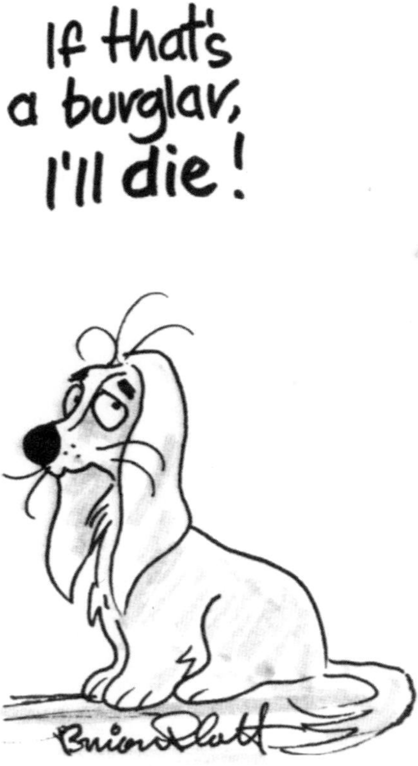
If that's a burglar, I'll die!
Brian Platt

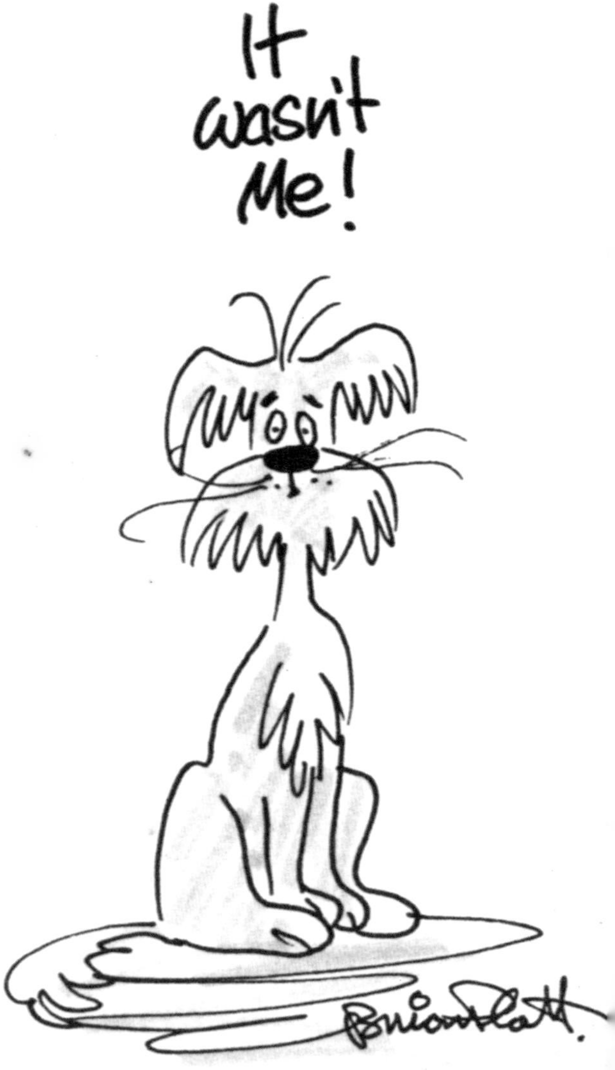
It wasn't Me!